# LEARN MATHS WITH FRACTIONS

By Hilary Koll & Steve Mills

Illustrated by Michael Buxton

First published in Great Britain in 2022
by Wayland
Copyright © Hodder and Stoughton 2022
All rights reserved

Editor: Julia Bird
Design: Collaborate
Illustrations: Michael Buxton

HB ISBN: 978 1 5263 1901 2
PB ISBN: 978 1 5263 1903 6

Wayland, an imprint of Hachette Children's Group
Part of Hodder and Stoughton
Carmelite House
50 Victoria Embankment
London EC4Y 0DZ

An Hachette UK Company
www.hachette.co.uk
www.hachettechildrens.co.uk

Printed in China

# Contents

| | |
|---|---|
| One half | 4 |
| Find half of a set | 6 |
| Mixed numbers | 8 |
| One quarter | 10 |
| Quarter turns | 12 |
| Halves and quarters | 14 |
| Thirds | 16 |
| Fractions that make wholes | 18 |
| Greater than or less than | 20 |
| Fractions of small numbers | 22 |
| Equivalence | 24 |
| Tenths | 26 |
| Twelfths | 28 |
| Glossary | 30 |
| Answers | 31 |

The words in **bold** are in the glossary on page 30.

# ONE HALF

Mo and his mum are going into town! Their first stop is the hairdresser.

Mo must sit still and behave while his mum has her hair done. She gives him a colouring book to keep him quiet!

In Mo's colouring book each picture can be split into two equal parts, called **halves**. Mo colours one half of each picture.

One half can be written as $\frac{1}{2}$ which is 1 out of 2 equal parts.

On the next page of Mo's colouring book, he must colour the flags in different colours, making one half-red and one half-yellow.

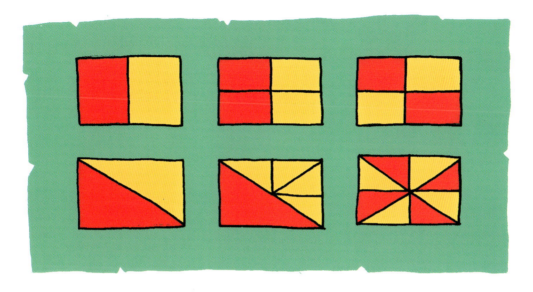

As long as there are the same number of equal parts that are red as yellow, it shows halves. Do you think Mo has coloured them correctly?

**Mo, with these rectangles, all except one is half-coloured red.**

**Which is the odd one out?**

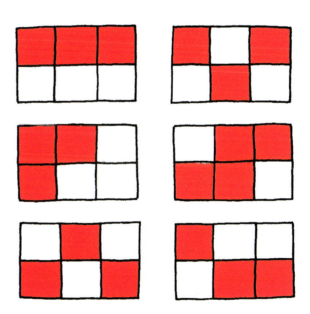

Mo correctly sees the rectangle with more red than white. Can you?

# FIND HALF OF A SET

As Mo behaved so well at the hairdresser, his mum takes him to the sweet shop as a reward.

They decide to buy a bag of sweets to share.

Sharing equally between 2 is the same as finding one half or $\frac{1}{2}$.

Split the sweets in each bag into two equal groups to find one half. How many will Mo get? The first one is done for you.

**Half of 4 is 2**

$\frac{1}{2}$ of 6 is ?

$\frac{1}{2}$ of 2 = ?

$\frac{1}{2}$ of 8 = ?

$\frac{1}{2}$ of 10 = ?

Lollies are being sold at half price in the shop. How much will each lolly cost in the sale? Find half the number of coins shown. The first one is done for you.

# Mixed NUMBERS

OOOH! LOTS OF PAIRS OF SHOES!

Mo needs some new shoes so the next stop is the shoe shop. Mo sees his favourite shoes in lots of different colours.

Mo counts the pairs of shoes in this row.

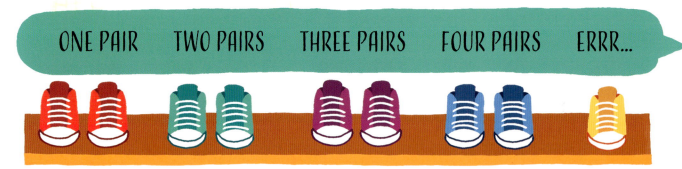

ONE PAIR   TWO PAIRS   THREE PAIRS   FOUR PAIRS   ERRR...

There is only half a pair of yellow shoes! So altogether in this row there are four and a half pairs. We write this as $4\frac{1}{2}$.

Mo counts the pairs again in halves.

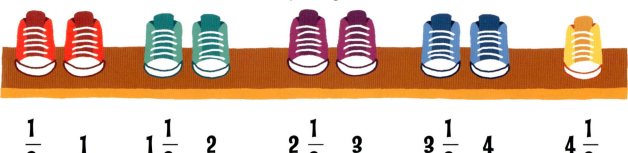

$\frac{1}{2}$   1   $1\frac{1}{2}$   2   $2\frac{1}{2}$   3   $3\frac{1}{2}$   4   $4\frac{1}{2}$

The shop assistant uses a tape measure to measure foot sizes. Mo's foot comes to $7\frac{1}{2}$ on it.

Can you point to $3\frac{1}{2}$, $6\frac{1}{2}$ and $8\frac{1}{2}$ on the tape measure?

Which number comes halfway between 9 and 10?

There are two halves in each whole. Mo, how many halves are there in $3\frac{1}{2}$?

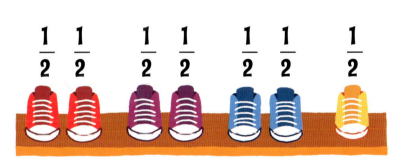

There are 7 halves in $3\frac{1}{2}$.

Can you see why?

# One QUARTER

Mo and his mum walk past a pizza restaurant and Mo sees some of his friends inside. He rushes in to say hello!

His friends offer Mo some of their pizza.

OOOH! MY FRIENDS!

Dizzy has a round pizza. He gives Mo one slice.

When a whole is split into four equal parts, each part is called **one quarter**.

One quarter can be written as $\frac{1}{4}$ which is 1 out of 4 equal parts.

Dizzy lets him have another slice, so Mo eats two quarters or $\frac{2}{4}$. Can you see that two quarters is the same amount as one half?

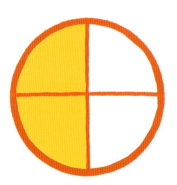

Sid cuts his pizza into quarters. Three slices are three-quarters or $\frac{3}{4}$.

The whole pizza has 24 slices of pepperoni altogether.

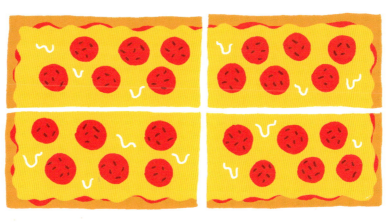

How many pieces of pepperoni are in:

| One quarter | Two quarters | Three-quarters |
|---|---|---|
| $\frac{1}{4}$ of 24 is ? | $\frac{2}{4}$ of 24 is ? | $\frac{3}{4}$ of 24 is ? |

Mo's clever friend Dizzy says:

> One quarter is half of one half!

Is Dizzy correct? Yes!

Mo says goodbye to his friends and leaves. But now he can't see his mum! Oh no! Where is she?

# QUARTER turns

OH NO! WHERE'S MUMMY?

Mo begins to worry. Where is his mum?

He turns to look down each nearby street to see if he can find her.

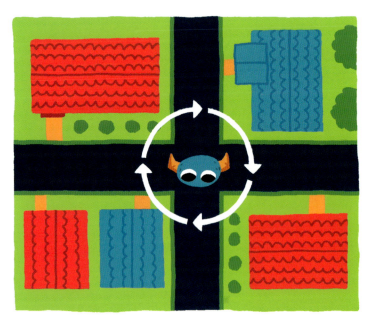

Each turn Mo makes to look down a street is a quarter turn.

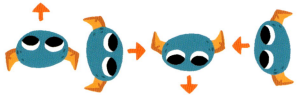

Mo turns four quarter turns and realises he has turned through a full turn.

Mo can't see his mum anywhere and is beginning to panic!

He turns through two more quarter turns and realises he has turned through a half turn.

 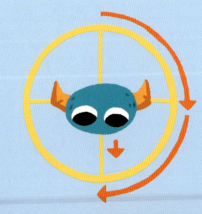

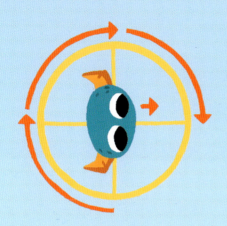

Then Mo remembers that his mum has always told him to wait under the big clock if they ever get separated.

He turns through three quarters of a turn and hurries towards the big clock.

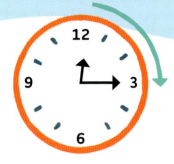

The clock shows the time is a quarter past twelve. The minute hand (the longer hand) has turned through one quarter of a turn from twelve o'clock. Mo waits under the clock for three quarters of an hour. What time does each clock show?

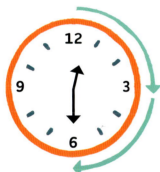
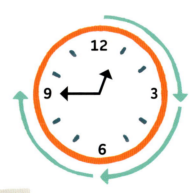
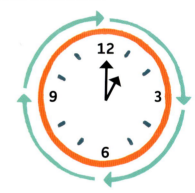

Mo, are these statements true or false?

$$\frac{1}{4} + \frac{1}{4} + \frac{1}{4} + \frac{1}{4} = 1 \text{ whole}$$

$$\frac{1}{4} + \frac{3}{4} = 1 \text{ whole}$$

TRUE?

Well done Mo. They are both true!

# HALVES AND QUARTERS

Mo has been waiting so long that he is getting bored. Next to the clock Mo notices a photo booth flashing.

He pops his head inside. The machine starts taking pictures of Mo!

A set of four photos come out of the machine. In one quarter of them Mo has his eyes shut!

**In what fraction of the set of photos can you see Mo's tongue?**

In what fraction of the set of photos can you see Mo's mouth?

In what fraction of the set of photos is Mo waving?

Can you give a different correct answer to the last question?

Four more photos come out of the machine.

Which fraction matches each?

Mo yawning

Both paws showing

Mo smiling

$\frac{1}{2}$

$\frac{1}{4}$

$\frac{3}{4}$

Mo holds both sets of photos in his paws.

He counts up that 4 of the 8 photos show him with both eyes open.

What fraction is this?

He counts up that 2 of the 8 photos show him with both eyes shut.

What fraction is this?

15

# THIRDS

There is still no sign of Mo's mum. Next to the photo booth is a shop selling badges. Mo loves badges and looks in the window, trying to decide which one he likes best.

Mo likes the badges that are split into three equal parts, like these.

He knows that we say halves when a whole is split into 2 equal parts and quarters when a whole is split into 4 equal parts.

We say **thirds** when a whole is split into 3 equal parts.

What part, or fraction, of each badge is one colour?

One third is written as $\frac{1}{3}$, two thirds is $\frac{2}{3}$ and three thirds (one whole) is $\frac{3}{3}$. What fraction of each of these badges is coloured? Count the number of equal parts carefully to help you decide.

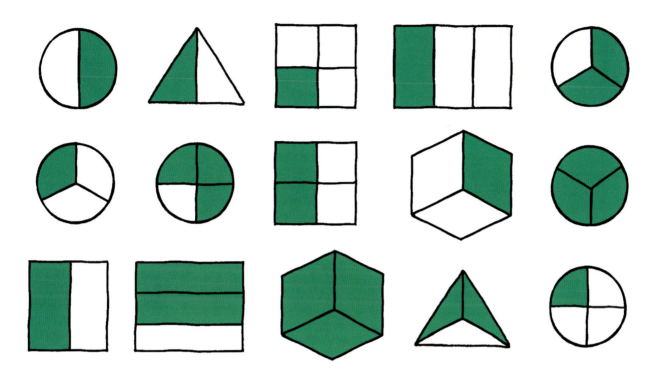

Mo, is it true that the number of equal parts in one whole is always the number on the bottom of the fraction?

UMM ...

Yes! The number down at the bottom of a fraction is called the **denominator**. It tells you how many equal parts the whole has been split into.

For thirds, the denominator is 3.

For quarters, the denominator is 4 and so on.

The top number, called the **numerator**, shows how many of those parts you are talking about, for example:

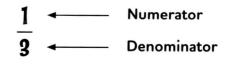

$\frac{1}{3}$ ← Numerator / Denominator

# Fractions that make WHOLES

Mo sees a small dog running around the shopping centre. It is lost, a bit like Mo!

Mo chases the dog, but it runs into a toy shop.

Mo follows the dog and sees it knock over a big pile of blocks. Oh no! The blocks are like slices of pie made from plastic.

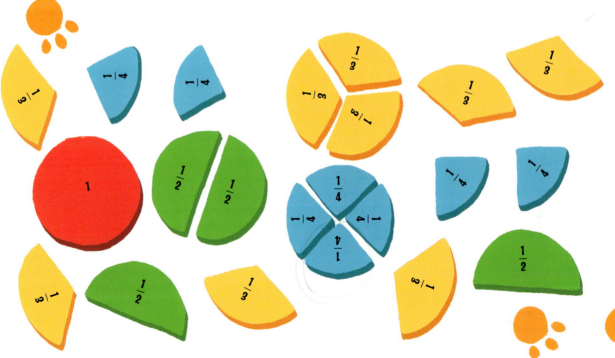

Mo quickly starts to put the pieces back together to make whole pies.

On the toy box is a list of all the pieces. How many whole pies are there altogether?

 whole  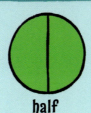 half   third   quarter

1 red whole — **1 whole**

4 green halves — $\frac{1}{2} + \frac{1}{2} + \frac{1}{2} + \frac{1}{2} =$ ? wholes

8 blue quarters — $\frac{1}{4} + \frac{1}{4} + \frac{1}{4} + \frac{1}{4} + \frac{1}{4} + \frac{1}{4} + \frac{1}{4} + \frac{1}{4} =$ ? wholes

9 yellow thirds — $\frac{1}{3} + \frac{1}{3} + \frac{1}{3} + \frac{1}{3} + \frac{1}{3} + \frac{1}{3} + \frac{1}{3} + \frac{1}{3} + \frac{1}{3} =$ ? wholes

Mo, which of these sets of fractions make exactly one whole?

UM ...

$\frac{1}{4} + \frac{1}{3}$   $\frac{1}{4} + \frac{3}{4}$

$\frac{2}{3} + \frac{1}{3}$   $\frac{1}{2} + \frac{1}{4}$

Mo takes the dog outside and finds its owner. The owner is so grateful he gives Mo a cap as a reward!

# GREATER THAN OR LESS THAN

Mo looks around and sees some young monsters trying to buy fruit and vegetables from a stall. Mo's mum has always told him to help others, so Mo offers to help them.

The pair explain that they want less than half a kilogram of some fruits and vegetables. Mo wonders if he can work out which of the fractions are more and which are less than half, and which are equal to one half.

Can you help the little monsters work out which bags to buy?

Which bags weigh one whole kilogram?

A fraction wall is a useful way of comparing fractions of different sizes.

Is $\frac{3}{4}$ greater than or less than $\frac{1}{2}$? Have a look at the wall below to help you.

Mo, which fraction in each of these pairs is larger?

$\frac{1}{4}$ or $\frac{1}{3}$  $\qquad$  $\frac{1}{4}$ or $\frac{1}{2}$

$\frac{2}{3}$ or $\frac{1}{2}$  $\qquad$  $\frac{3}{4}$ or $\frac{2}{3}$

Can you work it out with Mo?
Use the fraction wall to help you.

The little monsters thank Mo for his help and give him some apples as a thank you gift.

Well done Mo!

# FRACTIONS
## of small numbers

Mo remembers that he is still looking for his mum! There is a friendly-looking lady working at a florist's nearby and Mo goes to talk to her.

She is busy arranging flowers into different pots. Mo offers to help.

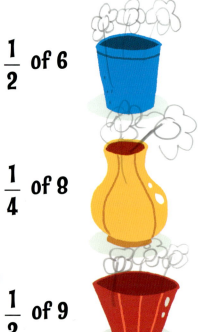

Put one half of these 6 flowers into the blue pot.

$\frac{1}{2}$ of 6

Put one quarter of these 8 flowers into the yellow pot.

$\frac{1}{4}$ of 8

Put one third of these 9 flowers into the red pot.

$\frac{1}{3}$ of 9

How many flowers will Mo put into the pot each time?

To find a fraction of a small number, try splitting them into equal groups. To find a half use 2 groups, for one quarter use 4 groups and for one third use 3 groups.

We can also use **division** to answer these questions.

$\frac{1}{2}$ of 10   is the same as   $10 \div 2$

$\frac{1}{4}$ of 20   is the same as   $20 \div 4$

$\frac{1}{3}$ of 15   is the same as   $15 \div 3$

If you know your times tables and division facts it is easy to find fractions of small numbers. Try these:

| | | |
|---|---|---|
| $\frac{1}{2}$ of 20 | $\frac{1}{4}$ of 20 | $\frac{1}{3}$ of 6 |
| $\frac{1}{2}$ of 24 | $\frac{1}{4}$ of 12 | $\frac{1}{3}$ of 12 |
| $\frac{1}{2}$ of 18 | $\frac{1}{4}$ of 16 | $\frac{1}{3}$ of 33 |

Correct!

The florist is very grateful for Mo's help so she gives him a small bunch of flowers!

# EQUIVALENCE

Mo sees someone who looks like his mum going into Mr Bond's cake shop. He follows her inside but it isn't his mum! Mo is so hungry that he just stares at all the cakes. His tummy is rumbling!

The owner of the shop, Mr Bond, is cutting a cake into slices. He is talking to his assistant and laughing.

> Would you like one half or two quarters of this cake?

His assistant laughs. Mo wonders why.

> I'd like three sixths of the cake please!

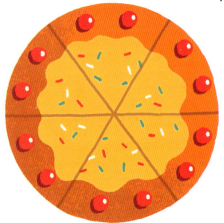

Mo looks at the cake. He knows thirds are made when splitting a whole into three equal parts, and guesses that **sixths** are made when splitting into six equal parts.

So $\frac{1}{6}$ is one slice, $\frac{2}{6}$ is two slices, $\frac{3}{6}$ is three slices, and so on.

$\frac{1}{2}$  $\frac{2}{4}$  $\frac{3}{6}$

Mo suddenly realises why Mr Bond and his assistant are laughing. Can you see why?

Fractions that look different can sometimes stand for the same amount. We say the fractions are **equivalent**, which comes from the word **equal**.

$\frac{2}{6}$ is equivalent to another fraction Mo knows.

$\frac{1}{2}$ $\quad$ $\frac{1}{4}$ $\quad$ $\frac{2}{4}$ $\quad$ $\frac{3}{4}$ $\quad$ $\frac{4}{4}$ $\quad$ $\frac{1}{3}$ $\quad$ $\frac{2}{3}$ $\quad$ $\frac{3}{3}$

$\frac{2}{6}$

Can you see that $\frac{2}{6}$ is the same amount of cake as $\frac{1}{3}$?

Find a fraction in the box above that is equivalent to each of these.

$\frac{4}{6}$  $\quad$ $\frac{4}{8}$  $\quad$ $\frac{2}{8}$  $\quad$ $\frac{6}{8}$

Mo, which of these pairs shows two equivalent fractions?

$\frac{1}{4} \quad \frac{2}{8}$ $\qquad$ $\frac{1}{2} \quad \frac{3}{6}$

$\frac{2}{3} \quad \frac{4}{6}$ $\qquad$ $\frac{1}{2} \quad \frac{4}{8}$

UM. ALL OF THEM?

That's right Mo!

Mo wishes he could have one half, two quarters, three sixths or four eighths of a cake! Any would be nice. He is really hungry!

# TENTHS

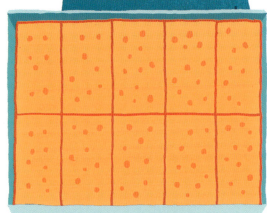

Mo asks Mr Bond if he has seen his mum. Mr Bond says he hasn't, but offers to help find her.

In the meantime, he gives Mo one slice of flapjack from the tray he has just sliced. Mo is very happy!

The tray of flapjacks has been cut into ten equal slices.

When a whole is split into ten equal parts, each part is called **one tenth** and is written as the fraction $\frac{1}{10}$.

This number line shows tenths up to one whole tray of flapjacks.

0   $\frac{1}{10}$   $\frac{2}{10}$   $\frac{3}{10}$   $\frac{4}{10}$   $\frac{5}{10}$   $\frac{6}{10}$   $\frac{7}{10}$   $\frac{8}{10}$   $\frac{9}{10}$   1  $\frac{10}{10}$

How many slices are there in half a tray?

Which fraction is equivalent to one half? $\frac{1}{2}$ is equivalent to $\frac{?}{10}$

Mo looks at the tray with his slice missing. How much of the tray is left?

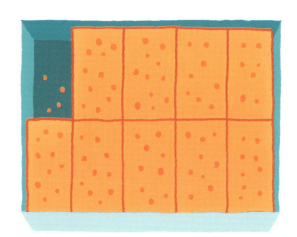

$$\frac{10}{10} - \frac{1}{10} = \frac{9}{10}$$

$$\frac{1}{10} + \frac{9}{10} = \frac{10}{10}$$

When adding or subtracting fractions with the same bottom number (denominator) only the numbers on the top (the numerators) change. For example,

$$\frac{5}{10} + \frac{2}{10} = \frac{7}{10}$$

The numbers on the bottom (the denominators) stay the same. That makes it easy to add and subtract fractions, Mo thinks!

Can you spot a mistake here though?

$$\frac{1}{10} + \frac{1}{10} = \frac{2}{10} \qquad \frac{10}{10} - \frac{2}{10} = \frac{8}{10}$$

$$\frac{3}{10} + \frac{3}{10} = \frac{6}{20} \qquad \frac{5}{10} - \frac{2}{10} = \frac{3}{10}$$

*not ten*

Mo suddenly hears his name being announced over the loudspeaker in the shopping centre. Mr Bond is asking Mo's mum to come to the shop. Mo suddenly feels very tired. He misses his mum and wants to go home now.

# TWELFTHS

Mo turns around and sees his mum running towards him! She looks very flustered and hasn't bought many things in the shops.

Mo gives her the bunch of flowers and the apples and shows her his new cap. His mum is very happy and relieved to see that Mo is okay.

Mo and his mum thank Mr Bond for his help. Mr Bond is so happy for them that he gives them a whole box of 12 cupcakes – Mo's favourite!

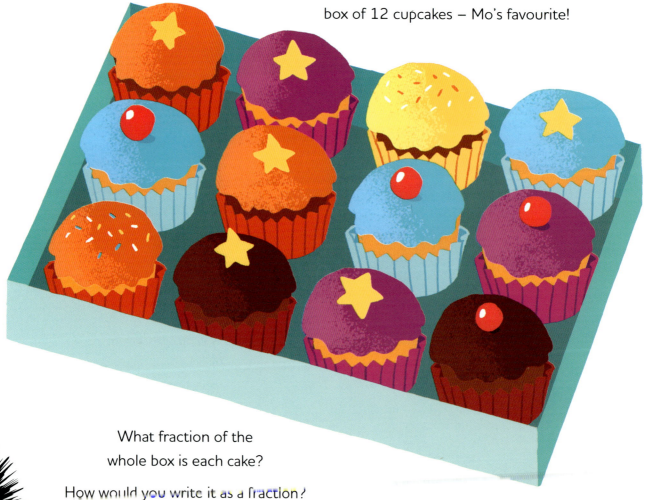

What fraction of the whole box is each cake?

How would you write it as a fraction?

In the car on their way home Mo looks at the colours and the decorations on the cupcakes.

Mo wonders how these can be written as fractions. Can you help him? The first one is done for you.

1 out of the 12 cupcakes is yellow.  $\dfrac{1}{12}$

6 out of 12 have stars on them.  $\dfrac{?}{?}$

4 out of 12 have cherries on top.  $\dfrac{?}{?}$

3 out of 12 are blue.  $\dfrac{?}{?}$

2 out of 12 are chocolate.  $\dfrac{?}{?}$

Can you think of a different fraction that is equivalent to each of these?

$\dfrac{6}{12}$  $\dfrac{4}{12}$  $\dfrac{3}{12}$

Mo tells his mum about all of his adventures, helping the florist, the little monsters and rescuing the dog. She tells him how proud she is of him for helping so many people. She says he can choose one of the cupcakes to eat, but when she looks round she sees Mo is already fast asleep!

# Glossary

**denominator**
the bottom number in a fraction that tells you how many equal parts the whole has been split into

**divide**
sharing things equally or into equal groups

**division sign**
the sign ÷ is used to show into how many equal groups something is being divided or to show how many are in each group

**equals**
the same amount as. The equal sign (=) shows what is on one side of the sign has the same value as what is on the other side

**equivalent**
having the same value. For example, $\frac{1}{2}$ is equivalent to $\frac{2}{4}$ or $\frac{5}{10}$ and so on

**fraction**
part of a number, set or object split into equal parts. If the numerator is smaller than the denominator, the fraction is called a proper fraction. If the numerator is larger than the denominator it is called an improper fraction

**half**
one out of two equal parts ($\frac{1}{2}$)

**halve**
to find one half, to divide things into two equal parts

**mixed number**
a number that has a whole number and a fraction, such as $2\frac{1}{4}$ or $1\frac{2}{3}$

**numerator**
the top number in a fraction that shows how many parts we have, for example $\frac{2}{3}$ stands for two thirds

**quarter**
one quarter ($\frac{1}{4}$) is one out of four equal parts, two quarters ($\frac{2}{4}$) is two out of four equal parts, three-quarters ($\frac{3}{4}$) is three out of four equal parts

**sixth**
one out of six equal parts ($\frac{1}{6}$)

**tenth**
one out of ten equal parts ($\frac{1}{10}$)

**third**
one third ($\frac{1}{3}$) is one out of three equal parts, two thirds ($\frac{2}{3}$) is two out of three equal parts

**twelfth**
one out of 12 equal parts ($\frac{1}{12}$)

# Answers

**Page 5**

Yes, Mo has coloured the flags correctly.

This rectangle does not show half since there are more red squares than white squares.

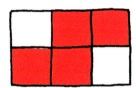

**Page 6**

$\frac{1}{2}$ of 6 is 3, $\frac{1}{2}$ of 2 = 1, $\frac{1}{2}$ of 8 = 4, $\frac{1}{2}$ of 10 = 5

**Page 7**

6 coins, 10 coins

8 coins, 7 coins, 9 coins

**Page 8**

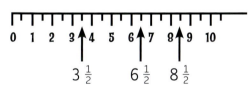

$3\frac{1}{2}$     $6\frac{1}{2}$     $8\frac{1}{2}$

$9\frac{1}{2}$

**Page 11**

$\frac{1}{4}$ of 24 is 6, $\frac{2}{4}$ of 24 is 12, $\frac{3}{4}$ of 24 is 18

**Page 13**

Half past 12, quarter to 1, 1 o'clock

**Page 14**

$\frac{1}{4}$

$\frac{3}{4}$

$\frac{2}{4}$ or $\frac{1}{2}$

**Page 15**

Mo yawning = $\frac{1}{4}$

Both hands showing = $\frac{3}{4}$

Mo smiling = $\frac{1}{2}$

$\frac{4}{8} = \frac{1}{2}$

$\frac{2}{8} = \frac{1}{4}$

**Page 16**

Each badge shows $\frac{1}{3}$ in one colour, $\frac{1}{3}$ in another and $\frac{1}{3}$ in another colour.

**Page 17**

$\frac{1}{2}, \frac{1}{2}, \frac{1}{4}, \frac{1}{3}, \frac{2}{3}$

$\frac{1}{3}, \frac{3}{4}, \frac{2}{4}$, or $\frac{1}{2}, \frac{1}{3}, \frac{3}{3}$ or one whole

$\frac{1}{2}, \frac{2}{3}, \frac{3}{3}$ or one whole, $\frac{2}{3}, \frac{1}{4}$

**Page 19**

There are 8 whole pies altogether.

4 green halves = 2 wholes

8 blue quarters = 2 wholes

9 yellow thirds = 3 wholes

$\frac{1}{4} + \frac{3}{4} = 1$ whole

$\frac{2}{3} + \frac{1}{3} = 1$ whole

## Page 20

$\frac{3}{4}$ is greater than $\frac{1}{2}$

$\frac{1}{4}$ is less than $\frac{1}{2}$

$\frac{1}{3}$ is less than $\frac{1}{2}$

$\frac{2}{3}$ is greater than $\frac{1}{2}$

$\frac{1}{3}$ is less than $\frac{1}{2}$

$\frac{2}{4}$ is equal to $\frac{1}{2}$

$\frac{1}{2}$ is equal to $\frac{1}{2}$

$\frac{3}{3}$ is more than $\frac{1}{2}$; it is equal to one whole.

$\frac{4}{4}$ is more than $\frac{1}{2}$; it is equal to one whole.

## Page 21

$\frac{3}{4}$ is greater than $\frac{1}{2}$

$\frac{1}{3}$ is greater than $\frac{1}{4}$

$\frac{1}{2}$ is greater than $\frac{1}{4}$

$\frac{2}{3}$ is greater than $\frac{1}{2}$

$\frac{3}{3}$ is greater than $\frac{3}{4}$

## Page 22

$\frac{1}{2}$ of 6 = 3

$\frac{1}{4}$ of 8 = 2

$\frac{1}{3}$ of 9 = 3

## Page 23

$\frac{1}{2}$ of 20 = 10, $\frac{1}{4}$ of 20 = 5
$\frac{1}{3}$ of 6 = 2

$\frac{1}{2}$ of 24 = 12, $\frac{1}{4}$ of 12 = 3
of 12 = 4

$\frac{1}{2}$ of 18 = 9, $\frac{1}{4}$ of 16 = 4,
$\frac{1}{3}$ of 33 = 11

## Page 24

They are laughing because $\frac{1}{2}$ is equivalent to (the same amount as) $\frac{2}{4}$ and to $\frac{3}{6}$.

## Page 25

$\frac{4}{6}$ is equivalent to $\frac{2}{3}$

$\frac{4}{8}$ is equivalent to $\frac{1}{2}$ or $\frac{2}{4}$

$\frac{2}{8}$ is equivalent to $\frac{1}{4}$

$\frac{6}{8}$ is equivalent to $\frac{3}{4}$

## Page 26

5 out of 10 slices is half a tray

$\frac{5}{10}$ is equivalent to $\frac{1}{2}$

## Page 27

The mistake is $\frac{3}{10} + \frac{3}{10} = \frac{6}{20}$ – it should be $\frac{3}{10} + \frac{3}{10} = \frac{6}{10}$ as the denominator (bottom number) shouldn't change when adding or subtracting fractions with the same denominator.

## Page 28

One twelfth or $\frac{1}{12}$

## Page 29

1 out of the 12 cupcakes is yellow $\frac{1}{12}$

6 out of 12 have stars on them $\frac{6}{12}$

4 out of 12 have cherries on top $\frac{4}{12}$

3 out of 12 are blue $\frac{3}{12}$

2 out of 12 have chocolate on them $\frac{2}{12}$

$\frac{6}{12} = \frac{1}{2}$, $\frac{4}{12} = \frac{1}{3}$, $\frac{3}{12} = \frac{1}{4}$